What would you be? in Ancient Rome

First published in Great Britain in 2023
by NQ Publishers, an imprint of Nextquisite Ltd.

Copyright © 2023 by Nextquisite Ltd

All rights reserved. Unauthorized reproduction, in any manner, is prohibited.

www.nqpublishers.com

www.nextquisite.com

Project Director Anne McRae
Art Director Marco Nardi

Illustrations Steph Marshall
Text David Owen
Editing Helen Woods
Picture Research Nicola Burns
Graphic Design Marco Nardi
Layouts Filippo Delle Monache

ISBN 978-1-912944-63-7

Printed in China

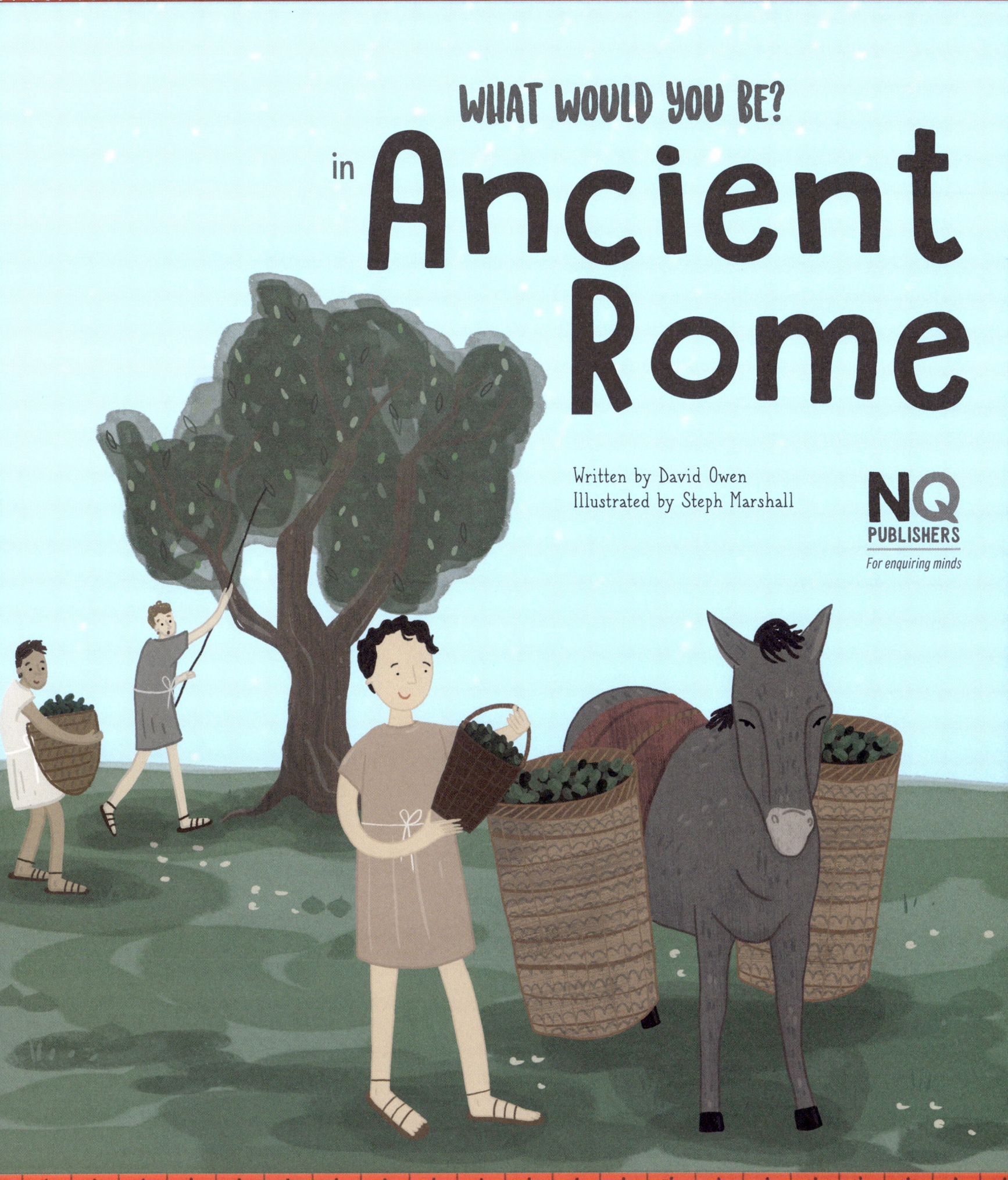
WHAT WOULD YOU BE?
in Ancient Rome

Written by David Owen
Illustrated by Steph Marshall

NQ PUBLISHERS
For enquiring minds

CONTENTS

LIVING IN ANCIENT ROME — 10
Timeline

ETRUSCAN TIMES — 12
The Origins of Rome

THE SENATOR'S SON — 14
The Roman Republic

YOUNG FARMERS — 16
Farming and Food

RUNNING THE EMPIRE — 18
The Roman Empire

A SOLDIER'S LIFE — 20
War and Weapons

KEEPING THE FLAME — 22
The Vestal Virgins

HAPPY SATURNALIA! — 24
Religion and Feast Days

THE APPRENTICE ENGINEER — 26
Roman Roads and Aqueducts

| THE FEARLESS CHARIOTEER | 28 |
| Sports and Entertainment | |

THE BIKINI GIRLS — 30
Roman Baths

THE TALENTED MAID — 32
Clothing and Jewellery

THE YOUNG LAWYER — 34
Education and Literature

THE ASPIRING GLADIATOR — 36
Daily Life in Ancient Rome

THE MERCHANT'S SON — 38
Trade and Banking

THE YOUNG WIFE — 40
Family Life

QUIZ TIME! — 42

INDEX — 44

TIMELINE

ROMAN KINGDOM
(753–509 BCE)
The time when Rome was ruled by kings.

ROMAN REPUBLIC
(509–27 BCE)
The time when Rome was ruled by elected officials.

ROMAN EMPIRE
(27 BCE–476 CE)
The time when Rome was ruled by emperors.

BYZANTINE EMPIRE (EASTERN EMPIRE)
(476–1453)
The time after the fall of the Western Empire. The Eastern Empire was ruled by emperors in Constantinople.

Dates in this book are shown as BCE (Before Common Era) and CE (Current Era). The Common Era starts with year 1.

753 BCE
Founding of the city of Rome
According to legend, Rome was founded in 753 BCE by Romulus and Remus, twin sons of Mars, the god of war. In reality, the city grew out villages built a few hundred years earlier.

27 BCE
The Roman Empire begins
The first 200 years of the Empire were a time of peace and prosperity. Great buildings like the Pantheon were built in the city of Rome, and the Empire's territories expanded.

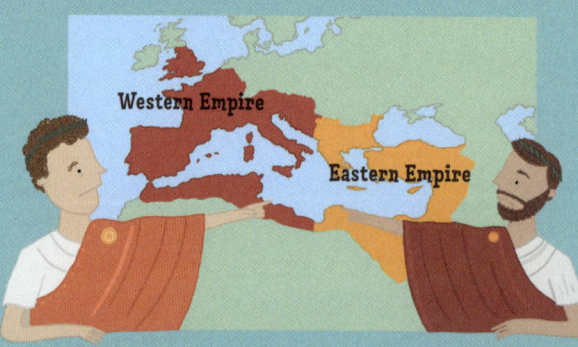

476 CE
Fall of the Western Empire
The last Roman Emperor was deposed in 476 by a Germanic king called Odoacer. The Western Empire collapsed, but the Eastern Empire continued for another thousand years. It was known as the Byzantine Empire.

LEO

509 BCE
Roman Republic begins
The last king is overthrown and Rome becomes a Republic ruled by elected officials called consuls.

285 CE
The Empire is split in two
The Emperor Diocletian divides the Empire in two. The Western Empire is ruled from Rome, while the Eastern Empire is ruled from Constantinople.

MAGNUS

LIVING IN ANCIENT ROME

TATIANA

SILVESTER

Close your eyes and imagine that you are walking through the bustling streets of ancient Rome almost 2,000 years ago. It's 140 CE and the Roman Empire is at its peak. With more than one million inhabitants, Rome is the largest city in the world, and possibly the noisiest! Huge crowds chanting their team slogans push you towards the chariot racing at the Circus Maximus. The Colosseum — the largest amphitheatre in the ancient world — and the magnificent, domed Pantheon temple are still newly built. Cook-shops line the streets and the tempting odours of delicious takeaways waft through the air, reminding you how hungry you are. If you have wealthy parents you will lead a safe and luxurious life, enjoying all the amusements a great city can offer. If you are from a poor family (as most people are), you will sometimes struggle, but you will always have food and entertainment provided for you by the emperor. Welcome to Rome — Caput Mundi – the capital city of the world!

Etruscans and Greeks

Before the rise of Rome, the Etruscans were the most powerful people in central and northern Italy, while the Greeks dominated the south and Sicily.

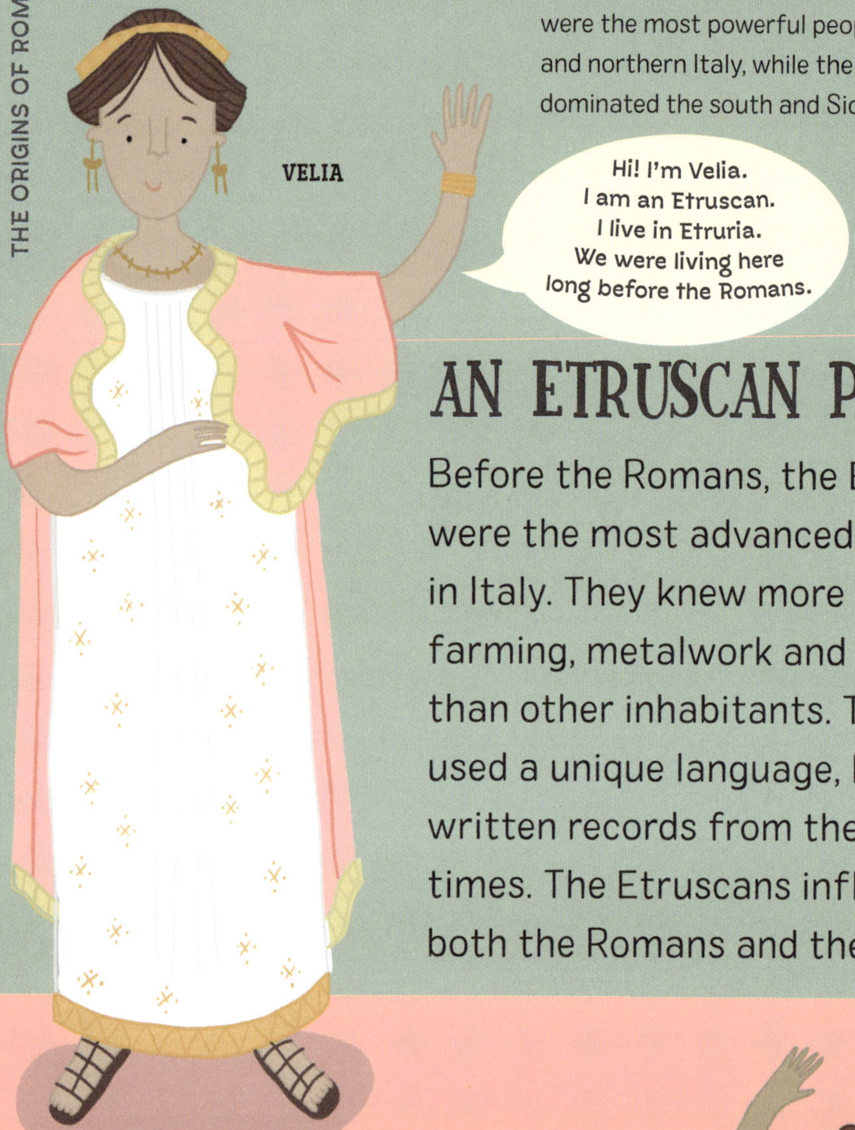

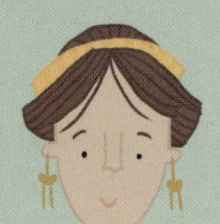

VELIA
Hi! I'm Velia. I am an Etruscan. I live in Etruria. We were living here long before the Romans.

AN ETRUSCAN PARTY

Before the Romans, the Etruscans were the most advanced people in Italy. They knew more about farming, metalwork and sculpture than other inhabitants. They used a unique language, keeping written records from the earliest times. The Etruscans influenced both the Romans and the Greeks.

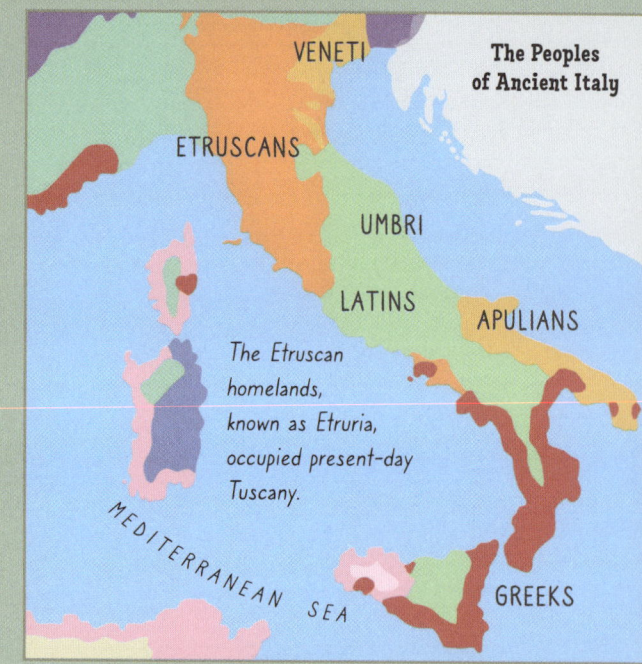

The Peoples of Ancient Italy
VENETI
ETRUSCANS
UMBRI
LATINS
APULIANS
The Etruscan homelands, known as Etruria, occupied present-day Tuscany.
MEDITERRANEAN SEA
GREEKS

Italians before Roman times

Many different peoples lived in Italy before the rise of ancient Rome. Over time, they joined Roman civilisation but traces of them remain in place names. The Umbri lived in modern Umbria, the Apulians in what is now Apulia, and the Veneti where Venice lies today.

An Etruscan banquet was like a big family party. The adults reclined on couches and chatted as they ate and drank. Children and pets sat on the floor.

A sophisticated culture

The Etruscans enjoyed fine food and wine, and they loved a banquet. Etruscan girls like Velia enjoyed a lot more freedom than other women in the ancient world. They went to banqueting parties, learned to read and write and could own property.

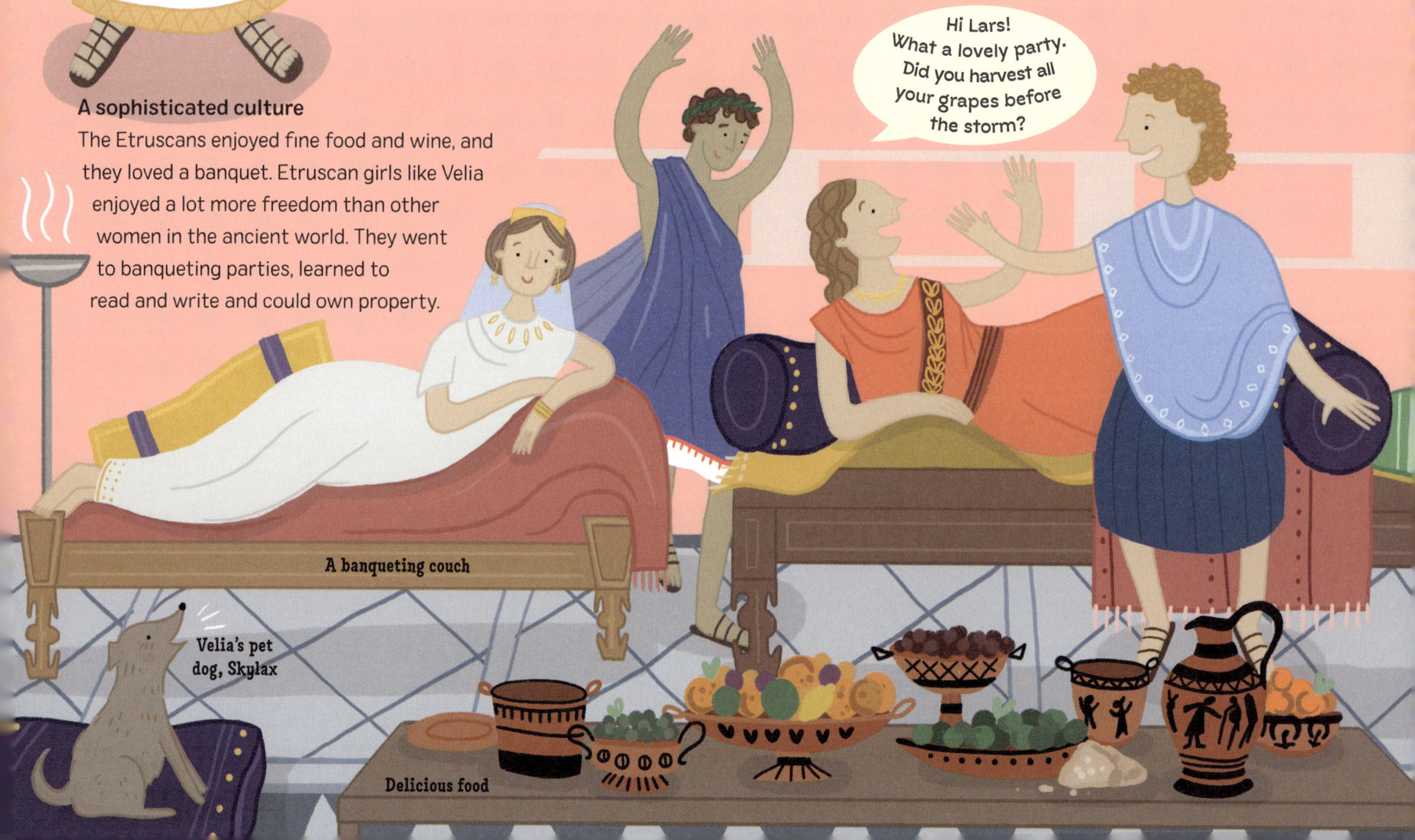

Hi Lars! What a lovely party. Did you harvest all your grapes before the storm?
A banqueting couch
Velia's pet dog, Skylax
Delicious food

THE FOUNDING MYTH OF ROME

According to legend, the Trojan hero Aeneas settled in Italy after the Greeks destroyed Troy. His descendants, the twin princes Romulus and Remus, were set adrift on the River Tiber by an evil king. They were rescued and raised by a She-Wolf. As adults, they overthrew the wicked king and founded Rome in 753 BCE.

This bronze statue of the She-Wolf feeding Romulus and Remus has been a symbol of Rome for over 2,500 years. It was made by Etruscan artisans.

She-Wolf

Romulus and Remus

THE ETRUSCAN KINGS

In the beginning Rome was a monarchy, ruled by seven kings. Romulus was said to be the first king. The last three kings were Etruscans. They were very unpopular and were eventually thrown out. They were replaced by the Republic of Rome, which lasted almost 500 years.

Etruscan writing

Many Etruscan men and women could read and write. We know from later Roman writers that they had a rich store of religious and historical texts, but the Etruscan writings themselves have been lost.

Etruscan was unrelated to any other language used in Italy at the time. It has been partly deciphered but only a few unimportant texts have been found.

Etruscan statue of a warrior

Etruscan artists made beautiful sculptures in terracotta and bronze. They also painted colourful frescoes.

A lot of Etruscan art was made to decorate tombs. Some of it has survived to the present day.

The Etruscans loved music, especially pipes and lyres. Guests would often dance at banquets.

Pipes

Lyre

"What do you think of these Romans?"

"They seem a bit uppity to me!"

Etruscan towns

There were at least 15 large Etruscan towns, some with populations of 30,000 or so. They were built on hilltops, which were easier to defend. The towns were connected by well-built roads and bridges.

THE SENATOR'S SON

During the Republic, Rome was ruled by two elected consuls. These men had the same power as a king, but they only served for one year. Rome grew rich and powerful during the Republic.

PETRUS

Hello! I'm Petrus. My Dad is a Senator. I sometimes go to hear him speak in the Senate.

The Punic Wars
The Romans fought many wars to defend and expand their territories. During the Punic Wars (264-146 BCE), they clashed with Carthage, an empire in North Africa, over control of trade in the Mediterranean Sea.

Hannibal, a general from Carthage, is famous for surprising the Romans with his war elephants.

Only Roman citizens could vote. Women, slaves and foreigners could not become citizens so they were excluded.

Patricians and plebeians
Society was divided into two classes: the patricians, who were wealthy, and the plebeians, or common people, who were not. At first, only the patricians could vote for state officials, but over time plebeians also gained voting rights.

A man drops his vote into a box during an election.

The Senate
The consuls appointed a group of advisors, called senators. They met at the senate where they discussed the important issues of the day.

Carthago delenda est! (Carthage must be destroyed!)

That's my Dad!

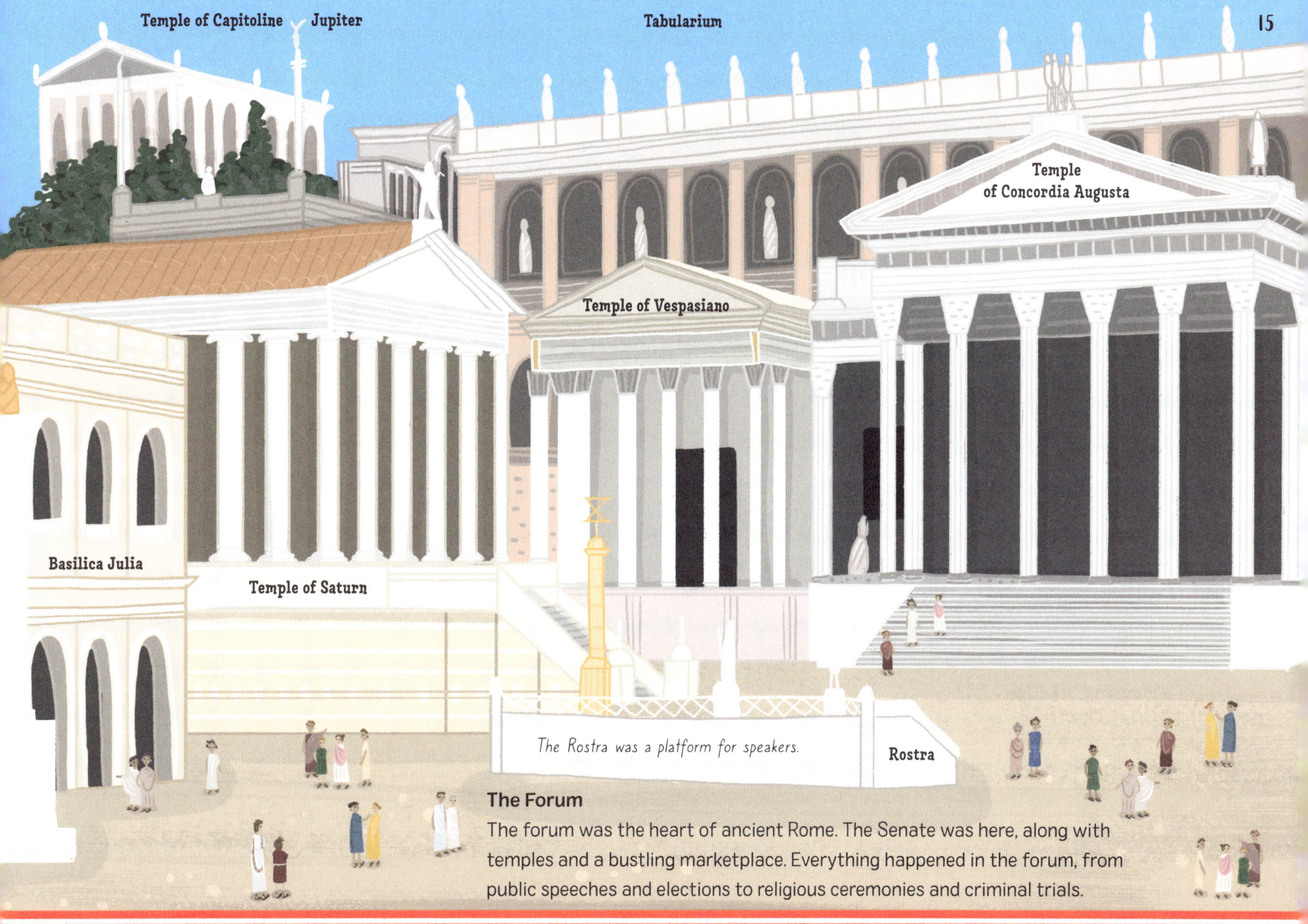

Temple of Capitoline Jupiter | Tabularium | Temple of Concordia Augusta

Temple of Vespasiano

Basilica Julia | Temple of Saturn

The Rostra was a platform for speakers. Rostra

The Forum
The forum was the heart of ancient Rome. The Senate was here, along with temples and a bustling marketplace. Everything happened in the forum, from public speeches and elections to religious ceremonies and criminal trials.

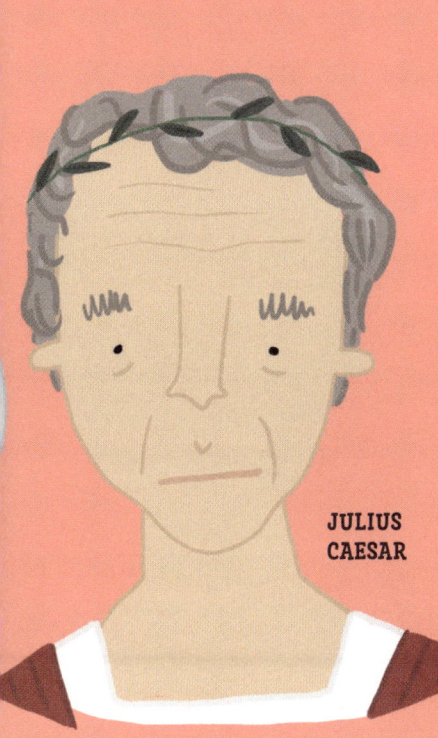

JULIUS CAESAR

Julius Caesar was a famous general and an able politician. In 45 BCE he convinced the people of Rome to make him their leader. The Senate did not agree and he was stabbed to death by a group of senators.

Caesar didn't rule for long but he made one change that we still use today. He introduced the "leap year," or adding an extra day every four years because an Earth year is slightly longer than 365 days.

THE END OF THE REPUBLIC
The Roman Republic ended for many reasons, including corruption, high crime and lack of money. Caesar's murder in 44 BCE was followed by years of civil war until his nephew and adopted son Octavian became the first Emperor of the Roman Empire. He changed his name to Augustus, which means "blessed by the gods."

Politics in ancient Rome was a dangerous game, with a lot of double-dealing, violence and murder.

YOUNG FARMERS

Farming was the most common job. It was the basis of Roman wealth and even more important than trade. In early times, most farms were small and run by the families that owned them. Later on, a lot of the land was divided into large estates run by wealthy landlords who had slaves and peasants to do the hard work.

Trampling the grapes with bare feet is fun but also really hard work.

Wine
Wine was a favourite drink and grapes were grown all over the Empire, even in Britain. Some grapes were eaten or dried into raisins, but most were made into wine.

LEO

Hi! I'm Leo. I'm 14 and I do most of the farm work. My little sister Iris works with me.

Olives
Olives were an important crop, mainly for their oil. Olive oil was used for cooking, but also as fuel for lamps and as the basis of perfumes, medicines and soaps. Demand became so great that vast olive groves were planted in Spain and North Africa and the oil was traded all over the Empire.

Leo lives on a small family farm. His father is often away on military campaigns so he runs the farm with his mother and sister.

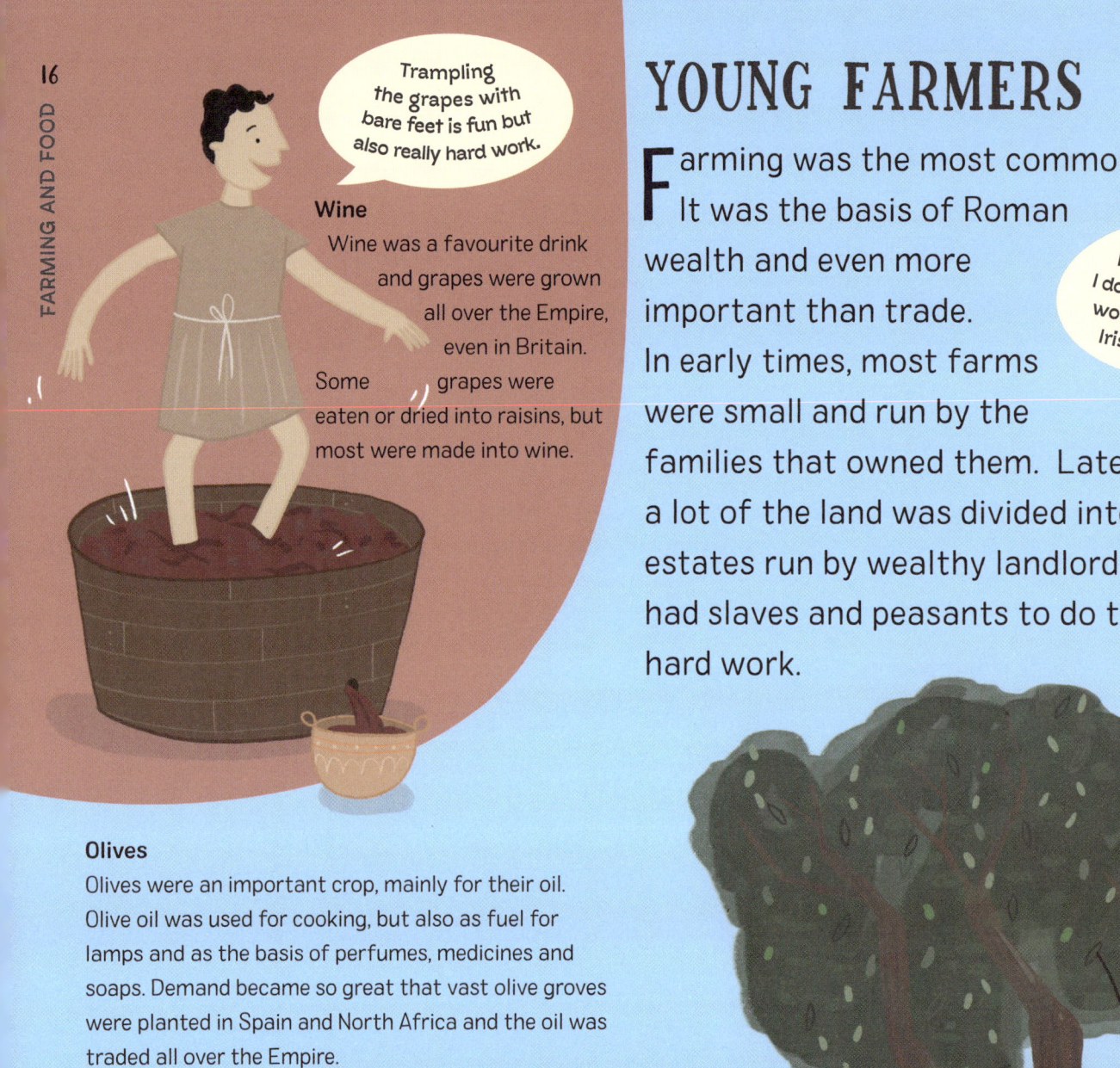

Olives were harvested in the autumn by hitting the trees' branches with sticks to knock the fruit to the ground. They were gathered into baskets and taken to the olive press.

"Hi, I'm Iris. I look after the farm animals."

IRIS

Pork was the Romans' favourite meat and pigs were kept all over the Empire. They were easy to feed in the winter and in the summer they foraged for themselves in the woods.

Animals

Farmers raised pigs, sheep and goats for their meat, wool and milk. Goat's and ewe's milk was made into tasty cheeses. Chickens and geese provided eggs and meat. Cattle were mainly kept as beasts of burden and for leather made from their hides. Animals were valuable property.

Pigs

Sheep

The Romans were good farmers. They stored seeds carefully and rotated different crops on their land to increase yields.

Crops

Grains like wheat and barley were widely grown to be made into bread and beer, which was what most ordinary Romans ate and drank, along with watered-down wine. Farmers grew fruit and nuts such as pears, figs and walnuts, as well as lots of different vegetables.

FOOD AND DRINK

Romans ate a broad range of grains, vegetables and fruit. They drank milk and ate cheese made from ewe's, goat's and cow's milk. They flavoured their foods with many different herbs and spices. Meat and fish were also common foods, although most people could not afford to eat them every day.

Fruit

Cereals

Sweet buns

Olives

Wine

Cheese

Sugar was unknown, but the Romans kept bees to make honey to sweeten food.

Garlic

Peas

Carrots

Vegetables

Onions

Bread

Poultry

Fish and seafood

EMPEROR LUCIUS

Hello! I'm Julia. My father is Emperor Lucius. He works so hard I hardly ever see him.

JULIA

RUNNING THE EMPIRE

Starting with Augustus in 27 BCE, the Roman world was ruled by a series of very powerful emperors. These men, backed by the fearsome Roman army, held absolute power. The senators and consuls of Republican times continued to exist for a while, but they no longer had any real power.

Job security
There were about 75 Roman emperors, 33 of whom were murdered or executed. It was not a job for the faint of heart!

Chief priest
The emperor was in charge of all religious matters. He was known as the "Pontifex Maximus," or chief priest. He was responsible for religious ceremonies, feast days, appointing Vestal Virgins, and much more.

Pax romana
The first 200 years of imperial rule were a golden age of relative peace as the empire grew in size and power. This time is called the *pax romana*, or "Roman peace."

After they died, Roman emperors were worshipped as gods.

The emperor organised animal sacrifices at temples on feast days and before military exploits to curry favour with the gods.

The emperor had his own private army, called the Praetorian Guard.

Commander-in-chief of the army
The emperor was the head of the Roman army. Many of the best emperors, such as Trajan and Hadrian, were closely involved in the army's activities, often spending years away from Rome on military campaigns.

THE WORST EMPERORS
Alongside the good Roman emperors, there were also some very bad ones. Here are some of the worst, and some of their most terrible deeds.

Nero (ruled 54-68 CE) became Emperor at 16 and was dead by his 30th birthday. He is known for being mad and cruel, murdering his own mother and two of his wives.

Caligula (ruled 37-41 CE) was very unpopular. He was cruel and possibly mad. At a gladiatorial contest, he threw a section of the audience into the ring and enjoyed watching them being mauled to death by wild animals.

Commodus (ruled 177-192 CE) thought he was a god. He executed his wife and whenever any of his advisors annoyed him, he had their families put to death.

Domitian (ruled 81-96 CE) was fearful and paranoid. He confiscated the property of people who opposed him and either exiled or executed them. In the end he was assassinated by his own staff.

Welfare and entertainment

The emperor was expected to organise entertainment like chariot races for the public to enjoy. In hard times, he had to find food for poorer citizens to stop them from rioting.

Every Roman town had an amphitheatre, a large arena where popular entertainments were held. The Colosseum in Rome was the largest.

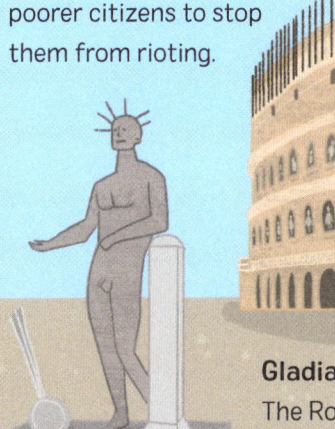

Gladiatorial contests

The Romans called these contests "games" but they were mainly fights between gladiators and animals and public executions of criminals. Blood and cruelty were what the Roman crowds liked to see.

"Yikes!"

The wild animals that fought in the arenas came from all over the empire and beyond. They included big cats such as lions and tigers, as well as bears, rhinos and crocodiles.

Decline of the Roman Empire

The empire slowly declined from about 300 CE, as groups of outsiders, such as the Huns and Vandals, invaded. Incompetent emperors and the arrival of Christianity led to the fall of the Western Empire in 476. The Eastern Empire continued as the Byzantine Empire until 1453.

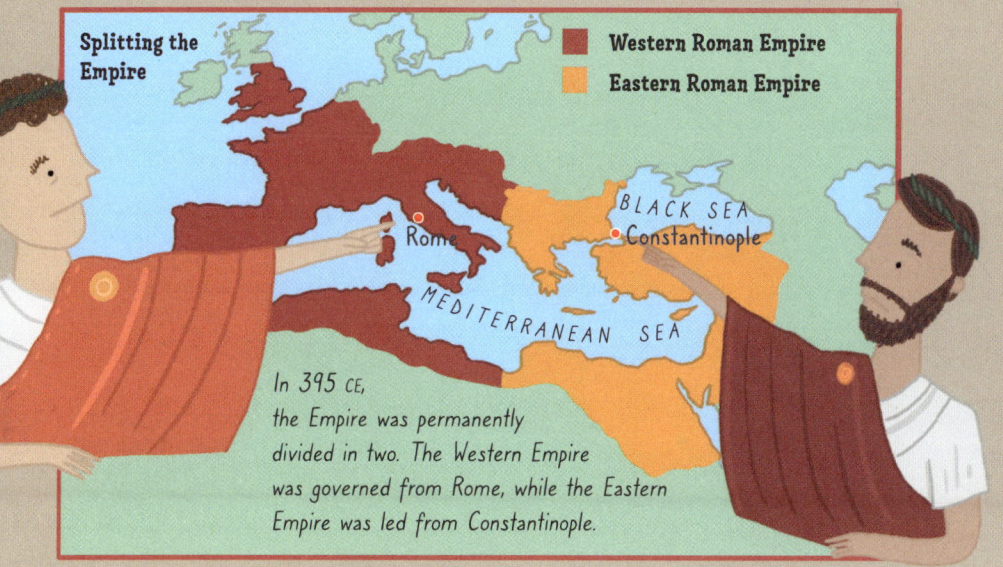

Splitting the Empire

- Western Roman Empire
- Eastern Roman Empire

In 395 CE, the Empire was permanently divided in two. The Western Empire was governed from Rome, while the Eastern Empire was led from Constantinople.

GREAT EMPERORS

The greatest emperors used their power to increase the size of the Roman Empire and to protect and help the people who lived within its borders.

Augustus (ruled 27 BCE–14 CE) was the first emperor. He restored peace and prosperity after many years of unrest.

Trajan (ruled 98–117 CE) expanded the empire to its greatest extent. He built spectacular bridges, roads and canals and provided food and education for the poor.

Hadrian (ruled 117–138 CE) was a popular emperor who travelled all over the empire, greatly strengthening the provinces. He built the wall in the north of England.

A SOLDIER'S LIFE

The army was the backbone of the Roman Empire. It was well-organised, disciplined and armed with the most advanced weapons of the day. Roman generals were respected and feared. As well as fighting to protect and extend Roman borders, soldiers also had to repair roads and bridges, build forts and supervise locals.

ABBAS

Hi! I'm Abbas. I'm stationed on Hadrian's Wall in Britain, although I come from Syria.

Armour

Shield

The army

The Roman army was the largest fighting force in the ancient world. It was the first army to have professionally trained, paid soldiers. It was divided into groups of 4,000 to 6,000 men, called legions. There were 30 legions stationed around the empire.

Like many Roman soldiers, Abbas was not a Roman citizen and he joined the army as an Auxillary soldier. After 25 years he (and all his sons) were awarded Roman citizenship.

The Roman Empire at its Greatest Extent in 117 CE

The Empire reached its greatest extent under the Emperor Trajan (98-117 CE).

Hadrian's Wall is 118 km (73 miles) long and took thousands of men four years to build. It was completed in 126 CE.

Hadrian's Wall

The Wall was built from sea to sea across the north of England on the orders of the Emperor Hadrian. It was meant to keep out the fierce Celtic tribes that lived to the north.

Local farmers

THE ART OF WAR

Battles were planned in advance by experienced generals. Sometimes the army never even fought. Instead they set up camp just outside the enemy town or territory and waited — often for weeks or months — until their foes surrendered, or starved to death.

Roman army fort

Tall siege towers were used to knock down city walls. A battering ram on the lower level delivered heavy blows. Soldiers hid inside, ready to attack.

Siege tower

Forts also had stables, stores, offices, workshops, baths, hospitals and a prison.

Bolt thrower

Forts were built wherever soldiers were stationed, especially along the empire's frontiers. Forts had barracks for the troops and houses for the officers.

Weapons Foot soldiers carried a short sword for hand-to-hand combat. They usually also had a shield and a long javelin-type sword. They wore armour for protection. Archers had bows and arrows.

War machines The Roman army was well equipped with war machines like the siege tower and the bolt thrower. Sometimes the enemy ran away when the Romans arrived!

The bolt thrower was used to launch bolts or stones at the enemy.

Battering ram

FLAVIUS

"Hi! I'm Flavius. I'm a Roman citizen. I signed up for 25 years."

Fighting machines
A Roman soldier was a well-trained fighting machine. He could march 30 km (20 miles) a day wearing all his armour and equipment. He could swim across rivers, build roads and bridges, and smash his way into forts.

Roman soldiers spent a lot of time training for battle.

As a Roman citizen, Flavius signed up as a Legionary. He was well trained, equipped and paid. At the end of his service he was given land to farm.

Duties
Soldiers weren't always at war. They also spent time patrolling conquered territories and building roads and forts. They helped to spread Roman culture.

FAMOUS VESTALS

We don't know much about the real Vestals, but there are some great stories.

Rhea Silvia, the legendary mother of Romulus and Remus. She was sentenced to death for breaking her vows, but was saved by the river god Tiber.

Aemilia was famous for throwing her fine linen cloak over the sacred fire when it went out. The flame miraculously rekindled.

Coelia Concordia was the last Chief Vestal. When the Emperor Theodosius closed the Temple she converted to Christianity.

KEEPING THE FLAME

The Vestal Virgins were powerful priestesses in ancient Rome. They guarded the City's sacred fire, never letting it go out. There were always six Vestals and when one left another was chosen in her place. Being a Vestal was a great honour, and the girls were selected from well-to-do families.

Vesta, the goddess of the hearth
The Vestal Virgins dedicated their lives to Vesta, the goddess of the hearth, home and families.

Here the goddess Vesta is shown with a donkey, one of her most common symbols.

Hi! I'm Lucia and this is Claudia. I'm 12 but Claudia is just six. It's her first day as a Vestal.

LUCIA

CLAUDIA

Young women became Vestal Virgins when they were six to ten years old and stayed for 30 years.

The Vestals collected water from a sacred spring. Even though they used a sieve to do this, no water was said to fall.

Duties and privileges
The Vestals had many duties but they also had privileges. They could vote and own property and had seats of honour at ceremonies. Harming a Vestal was punishable by death.

The young women lived together in the beautiful House of the Vestals. Many became firm friends and had wonderful times together.

House of the Vestals

Temple of Vesta

Initiation
The Vestals were chosen by the chief priest. A special ceremony was held when a new Vestal joined the cult.

The Chief Priest led the chosen girl away from her family with the words: "*I take you, amata (beloved), to be a Vestal priestess, who will carry out sacred rites which it is the law for a Vestal priestess to perform on behalf of the Roman people...*"

We keep the sacred fire burning in the Temple of Vesta in the forum.

After 30 years a Vestal could retire with a generous pension and a prominent position in society.

The sacred flame
The Vestals' main duty was to keep the sacred flame of Rome alight. The Romans believed that if the fire went out it would mean that the gods were no longer protecting the city, and it could be destroyed.

HAPPY SATURNALIA!

The Romans loved to celebrate religious occasions with feast days and fun. Saturnalia was the biggest festival. It was held from 17-23 December, but there were many other feast days too. Public holidays were paid for by the state with parades, street parties and games laid on.

"Io Saturnalia! I'm Diana and this is my little sister Rhea. Today is a huge party in Rome."

DIANA

RHEA

Gift giving
People exchanged gifts during Saturnalia. Candles were a common choice, and very useful in the short winter days.

On the last two days of Saturnalia people gave each other little animal statues made of wax or clay. They were called "sigillaria."

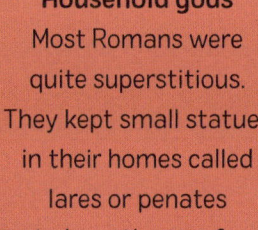

Sigillaria

"Io Saturnalia! Happy Holidays!"

"Io Saturnalia!" was a common greeting during this big winter festival. It was a bit like saying "Merry Christmas!" or "Happy Holidays!" today.

THE KING OF SATURNALIA

Household gods
Most Romans were quite superstitious. They kept small statues in their homes called lares or penates to keep them safe.

A household Lar

Saturnalia
This festival was held in honour of Saturn, the god of agriculture, time, wealth and war. In Rome, the festival was celebrated with a sacrifice at the Temple of Saturn in the forum. This was followed by a public banquet. During Saturnalia, the norms of Roman life were reversed, with masters waiting on their slaves and merrymaking in the streets.

A King of Saturnalia was elected during the festivities. He wore a special crown of laurel and directed the celebrations.

The Roman calendar

The earliest Roman calendar had ten months, running from March until December. During the Republic, two winter months were added — January and February.

Gods and goddesses

The Romans worshipped many gods and goddesses. Over time, local Roman gods became associated with the Olympians (the 12 famous Greek deities). The Romans adopted gods and religious practises from all over their empire.

A Roman calendar stone

Three main gods

The Capitoline Triad were the three most famous gods. They were Jupiter, the King of the gods, his wife Juno, protector of the state, and her daughter Minerva, the goddess of wisdom.

JUPITER **JUNO** **MINERVA**

TEMPLES

Roman temples were dedicated to a god or goddess or a famous person. They were a place for prayer and offerings, as well as sacrifices, usually of sheep.

The Pantheon in Rome is a famous temple dedicated to all the gods. It still stands today and shows what skilled architects the Romans were.

The Maison Carrée in Nimes, France, is a beautiful rectangular temple. It was built by General Agrippa in memory of his sons who died young.

Most temples were inspired by Etruscan and Greek architecture and were rectangular in shape. But the Romans also built some elegant **circular temples.**

THE APPRENTICE ENGINEER

The Romans were good at practical things, like building roads, bridges and drains, and making tools and machines. At first their knowledge came from the Greeks, but they soon surpassed them.

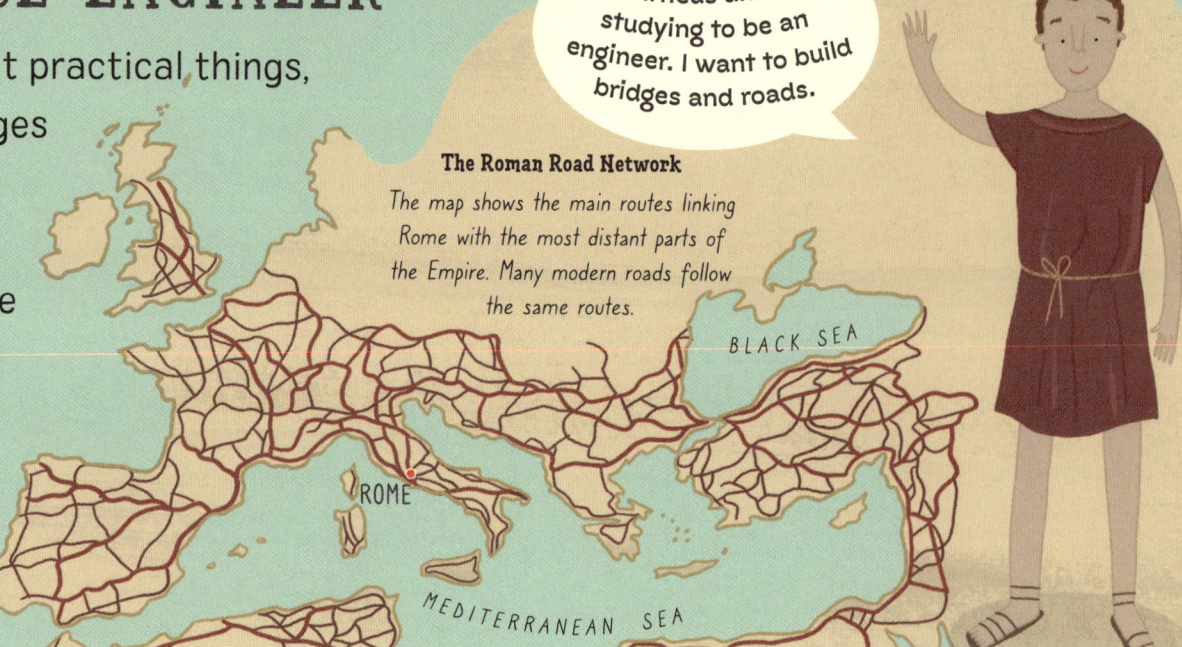

Greetings! I'm Atticus and I'm studying to be an engineer. I want to build bridges and roads.

ATTICUS

The Roman Road Network
The map shows the main routes linking Rome with the most distant parts of the Empire. Many modern roads follow the same routes.

All roads lead to Rome
The Roman army built a vast network of roads that linked Rome to its provinces. It helped the free movement of armies, people and goods all across the empire.

Travel
The roads were built by the army as they extended the boundaries of the empire. Merchants, messengers and travellers all used the roads.

Horses, donkeys, mules and oxen were used to pull vehicles. Animals were fed or exchanged at rest stops along the way.

Vehicles
Most Romans walked everywhere, but a few had carriages, carts or chariots that bounced and bumped their way over the cobblestones.

How roads were built
Road builders began by marking parallel tracks and then digging down between them. They filled this trench with layers of sand, lime, clay, stones, and fragments of terracotta. They laid wide flint or lava stones on top to create a smooth surface.

Groma

Roman roads were expertly engineered.

The engineer is using a Roman surveying instrument called a "groma" to make sure the road is straight and level.

Rounded stone arches were the most recognisable feature of Roman aqueducts.

Rome had eleven aqueducts bringing water from up to 92 km (57 miles) away.

"Look at the arches, Atticus. I will show you how to build them."

Aqueducts
The Romans built aqueducts to carry fresh water into towns and cities. They were an amazing feat of engineering. Some had tiers of rounded stone arches one on top of the other.

Drains
The Romans built drains under their cities to carry away rainwater and sewage. The same technology was used to build public baths and toilets.

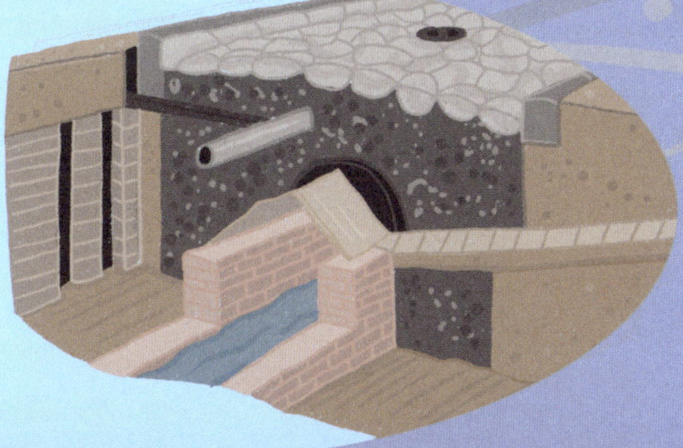

Luxurious Roman villas had underfloor heating.

Water power
Large watermills were built to crush grain into flour. Water from a river was channelled through the mill where it flowed over a series of water wheels, providing the power to turn the grindstones.

The use of watermills meant that the Romans could produce bread on an industrial scale.

Watermill

ROMAN ENGINEERING SKILLS
The Romans were famous for their engineering skills. Many of the structures they built are still standing.

Roads: The first major road, called the Appian Way, was built in 312 BCE. By the 5th century CE there were 400,000 km (250,000 miles) of Roman roads.

Arches: The arch was the basis of Roman architecture. It allowed them to build bigger buildings, longer roads and better aqueducts.

Bridges: Were built in stone with circular arches. They were stronger and lasted longer than wooden bridges.

Tunnels: The Romans built tunnels to carry water to towns, and to divert rivers and drain lakes to make way for farms.

Mills: Watermills were used to grind flour, but they were also used in mines to process ore and to polish gems.

Spectators were lifelong supporters of their favourite team, much as football fans are today.

White team Blue team Green team Red team

THE FEARLESS CHARIOTEER

The Romans loved sports and chariot racing was their favourite. On race days the streets of Rome were empty, as everyone was at the forum. The charioteers, who were often slaves or men from poor families, became immensely rich and famous. It was a very dangerous sport.

The four teams
There were four rival teams in Rome, named for their colours: the Whites, the Reds, the Greens and the Blues. Charioteers often switched teams, going to who paid them the most.

The charioteers wrapped the reins around their waists. They carried a dagger to cut themselves free if they crashed.

Whip

Leather helmet

Leather straps

Reins

Shaft

Wheels with bronze or iron for strength

Hello, I'm Felix. I'm 10 years old and I'm going to be the most famous charioteer of all.

FELIX

Like many charioteers, Felix is a slave boy. He dreams of being rich enough to buy his freedom, as his master did.

Hay

Members of the crowd often came to blows. One emperor had 12 people executed for shouting rude comments about his team.

pillar

Pillars

Tribuna

Racing ground

Entrance

TOP CHARIOTEERS

The top charioteers earned more than modern footballers. One charioteer, called Gaius Appuleius Diocles, was the wealthiest athlete in the history of sport. If you convert his earnings into today's money, he had winnings of more than 12 billion pounds!

The Circus Maximus
In Rome, the races were held at the Circus Maximus. There was seating for 250,000 spectators. Eight races were held each day. Each race was seven laps long and took about 15 minutes. Deadly accidents took place at the sharp corner in front of the Tribuna.

The best horses came from Africa and Spain. They were very brave.

One of Felix's jobs was to throw cooling water over his master's chariot as it swung by.

Up to three chariots from each team competed in each race. They worked together to ram their opponents or break their axles.

Chariots were usually pulled by teams of four horses, but sometimes there were only two, or up to ten.

Acrobats like Felix's friend Magnus performed between races, often riding on wild boars or lions.

Giddy-up!

MAGNUS

Wild boar

THE BIKINI GIRLS

Even small Roman towns had public baths. People came every day to bathe and exercise, but the baths were also a centre of social life. People stayed to gossip and have fun. In large city baths, there were places to meet friends and eat together.

LIVIA

SABINA

Hi, I'm Livia and this is my friend Sabina. We work at the Baths of Caracalla. I work in a snack bar while Sabina is a masseuse.

Isn't that relaxing, madam? The massage oil has lavender in it.

Mmmmm!

After work, Sabina and Livia put on their bikinis and play ball in the exercise court. Before going home, they have a swim to cool down.

The masseuse
Most baths had separate areas or times for men and women. Sabina works in the women's section of the baths where she massages wealthy Roman ladies with perfumed oils.

The Romans believed that exercise and sport were good for you and that a healthy body naturally led to a healthy mind and general well-being.

The Baths of Caracalla
The Baths of Caracalla in Rome were magnificent. They covered 62 acres (25 hectares) and could hold up to 1600 bathers at a time. On average, 6,000 to 8,000 bathers came every day.

There were hundreds of baths in Rome. Wealthy citizens often built heated baths at home, but they still went to the larger baths to meet people.

Tepidarium (warm-water bathing hall)

Caldarium (hot-water bathing hall)

Library

Shops

Unheated swimming pool

Frigidarium (cold-water bathing hall)

Changing rooms

Exercise court

An amazing complex
The Baths of Caracalla were very lavish. They were built of marble and imported Egyptian granite. The floors were covered in beautiful mosaics and the interiors were lined with statues. There were two libraries, gardens, shops and places to eat.

The baths were a great place to meet friends and catch up.

After exercising and before a bath, the Romans would rub olive oil into their skins. Then they scraped it off with a special tool called a strigil.

A social hub
The baths were a great place for Romans to meet and mingle. Business deals were agreed, marriages arranged and friendships made and lost when they gathered to bathe and gossip.

Heating the baths
The earliest heated baths used water from hot springs. Later, the Romans built the hot bathing halls over rooms where a furnace could be lit to burn wood to heat the water and the bathing area.

A lot of people worked at the baths, keeping them clean, heating the water and serving food to all the visitors.

Fast food
Ancient Romans often bought their lunch from snack bars known as *thermopolia*. The word means "hot things" and they could choose from a range of hot and cold ready-to-eat dishes including meat, fish, eggs, sausages, vegetables, lentils and cheese.

Often there was a place to sit and eat the food so it was very like going to a cafe or fast food place today.

Hi Livia! I'd like chicken and lentils today please. And some spinach.

The thermopolium was often just a small shop in the street. It had marble counters with holes in them for the food.

THE TALENTED MAID

Fashion and body care were important to the Romans. They went to public baths most days to exercise and bathe. People liked to dress well and to style their hair according to the latest fashion. If they could afford it, they also wore jewellery and perfume.

Hi, I'm Tatiana. I'm a slave. I work as a maid for a rich Roman woman. She is kind but I am not free.

TATIANA

Slavery
There were a lot of slaves in ancient Rome. They were usually people who were captured during a war. Slaves were bought and sold at markets. They had no rights but were sometimes able to gain their freedom.

Tatiana was captured by the Roman army during a battle near her home in Dacia (modern-day Romania). She was sent to Rome where she was sold to a wealthy Roman family.

Laws against extravagance
Many Romans loved glamorous outfits. In some periods, censors passed laws to stop people from wearing overly luxurious clothing and jewellery.

Tatiana has great taste in clothing, hair and jewellery. She helps her mistress to look stunning and soon gains a following among her wealthy Roman friends.

Wealthy Roman women often had several maids to help them dress and do their hair.

Perfume and cosmetics
Cosmetics were made at home from plants, insects, shellfish and other natural materials. Perfume was made using flowers and spices, usually with the addition of oil.

The use of cosmetics became popular among well-born women during Imperial times.

Perfume jar

Spice jar

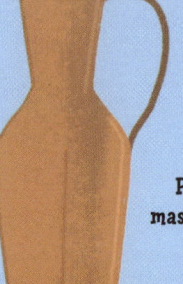
Perfumed massage oil jar

Hairstyles
Women wore their hair long. Styles differed according to age and status. Married women wore their hair up, mostly tied back in simple knots.

Elaborate styles
Fashions changed, but in some periods wealthy women wore their hair in very tall piles of curls!

Simple styles
Ordinary women wore simpler, easy-to-care-for styles. They often wore hair bands.

Men's hairstyles
Men wore their hair short and were clean-shaven, although some wore neatly-trimmed beards.

Men's clothing

Roman boys and men wore short-sleeved tunics. They varied in length from just above the knees to the ankles. They often wore a belt at the waist. When it was colder, men wore a variety of different cloaks.

When clothes needed cleaning they were usually sent out to a laundry where they were washed in a mixture of animal or human urine and water. If that sounds gross, you'll be delighted to know that the Romans also used urine as a mouthwash and teeth-whitener!

Well-to-do men wore a toga outside the house. It was a long piece of cloth wrapped around the wearer according to the latest style.

Girls wore knee-length tunics with a cloak for extra warmth in winter.

"Wow! You look great. Who did your hair?"

Women's clothing

Married women wore an ankle-length *stola*, tied at the waist and below the breasts and worn over a shift or petticoat. Sometimes they wore a *palla* (cloak) on top. It was a rectangle of cloth, usually draped over one shoulder. It could also be pulled over the head. They wore leather sandals or shoes.

"Free at last! I'm happy now."

Freedom!
One day, Tatiana's mistress decided to free her. She helped her to set up her own shop where Tatiana could advise women on dress, jewellery, hair and make-up.

JEWELLERY

Women wore more jewellery than men. Local craftsmen made beautiful items, but the rich often bought fine gold jewellery with precious gems imported from the Middle East and India.

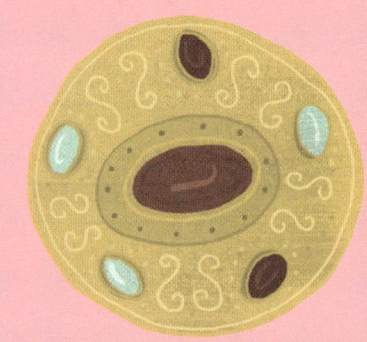

Brooches The Romans didn't have buttons, zips or velcro as we do today. They used brooches to hold their clothes in place.

Types of jewellery Precious stones such as opals, emeralds, diamonds, topaz and pearls were set as earrings, bracelets, rings, brooches, necklaces and tiaras.

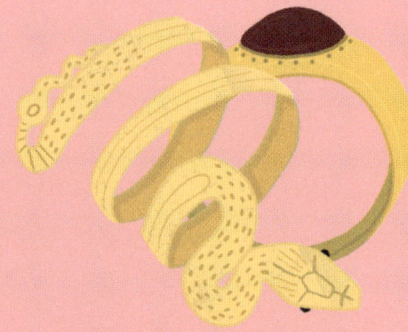

Men and children sometimes wore rings too. A string of beads often included a small amulet (charm) to guard the wearer against evil.

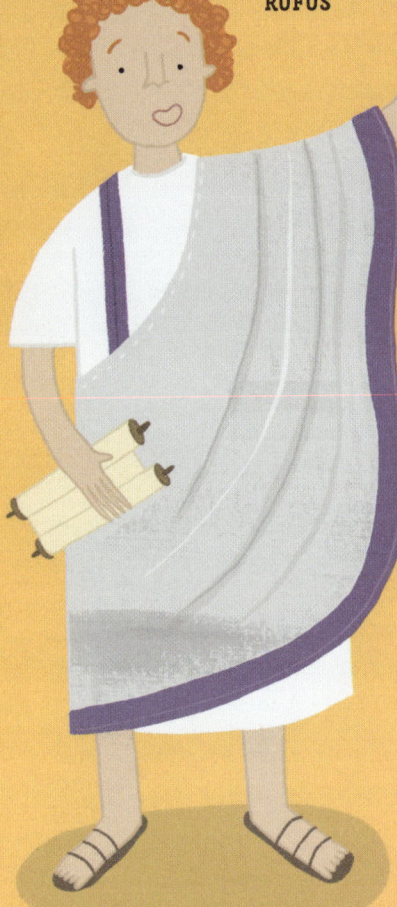

RUFUS

Greetings! I'm Rufus. I'm training to be a lawyer. I have to study rhetoric and law.*

*Rhetoric is the art of speaking or writing in an effective and persuasive manner.

Women's education
Most Roman women were not taught to read and write. A few girls from wealthy families were given an education by private tutors, but only if their family encouraged and helped them.

THE YOUNG LAWYER

During the Republic, wealthy Roman children were usually educated at home by tutors or family members. By the time the empire began, schools had been set up for well-off Roman boys. Most girls didn't go to school, although some received tutoring at home.

Schools
Roman boys started school at the age of seven. At their first school they learned reading, writing and basic mathematics using an abacus. If they did well, they could go on to more advanced schools, where they studied public speaking and the writings of famous philosophers and scientists.

What did Cicero write about?

Politics! Philosophy!

History! Law!

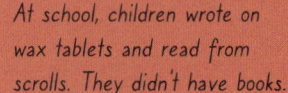

At school, children wrote on wax tablets and read from scrolls. They didn't have books.

Boys who studied hard and became scholars learned Greek as well as Latin. Many went to Greece to complete their studies.

Many teachers and tutors were slaves captured in Greece. They had good educations which they passed on to Roman children.

EDUCATION AND LEARNING

Justice and laws

The Romans developed a complex system of laws. Many of their ideas are still present in our modern legal systems, especially in Europe.

The earliest laws in Rome are from 449 BCE. Known as the "Twelve Tables," they were hung in the forum for all to see.

Rome was the capital city of the Roman Empire. This sign says "ROMA CAPUT MUNDI" which means Rome, Capital City of the World.

"You are guilty of stealing two sacred chickens from the temple. You must pay for eight new chickens!"

The courts were in the forum. Magistrates listened as lawyers presented their clients' cases then made a decision to resolve the dispute.

Lawyers
Lawyers began practising openly in Roman times and charging a fee for their services. They were expected to study and know the law. By late Roman times, a young lawyer like Rufus could expect to spend at least four years learning the ropes.

Sacred chickens
Priests in ancient Rome raised special sacred chickens to read omens and tell the future.

FAMOUS WRITERS, THINKERS AND SCIENTISTS

There were many great Roman historians, scientists and writers. They left a large body of work that has been studied ever since. It helps us to know about the ancient Roman world, and also the Greeks who preceded them.

Latin
The Romans spoke Latin, a language that was originally used by a small group of people living near Rome. As the Romans became more powerful, Latin spread first in Italy and then throughout the empire.

Cicero (106–43 BCE) was a great lawyer, writer and politician. He lived through the last days of the Republic. His writings tell us a lot about those turbulent times.

Virgil (70–19 BCE) Was Rome's greatest poet. His most important work, the *Aeneid*, tells the story of the legendary founding of Rome.

Livy (59 BCE–17 CE) was an historian who wrote a huge history of Rome, from its founding up until the early days of the empire.

Hypatia (around 350–415 CE) was a mathematician, philosopher and astronomer. She lived in Alexandria, Egypt, where she was a great teacher and a wise counsellor.

THE ASPIRING GLADIATOR

Rome was a bustling, noisy place to live. The streets were lined with hundreds of craftsmen's workshops and rang with the clang of blacksmiths' hammers, the roar of glassblowers' furnaces and the shouts of traders advertising their wares.

Hi! I'm Marius. I'm learning to be a butcher in my Dad's shop. But I dream of being a gladiator....

MARIUS

Marius' dream was not unrealistic. Many top gladiators came from poor families.

Blacksmiths made iron tools and steel weapons.

Craftsmen and workers
There were thousands of workshops scattered across Rome. They were often small family businesses with shops attached so that they could sell the things they made directly to the public.

Metal workers
The Romans imported metal ores from all over the empire and beyond. Skilled craftsmen smelted the metals in furnaces and made a wide range of products, from luxury items such as silver bowls and gold jewellery to everyday things like copper bowls.

CLOTH MERCHANTS

I'd like the red silk, please.

Cloth
Many Romans spun and wove their own clothing at home, but wealthier people bought it from craftspeople and importers.

BUTCHERS

Butchers
Often butchers were the farmers who raised the animals they sold as meat. But in large towns like Rome, there were high-end butchers selling meat they bought from abattoirs.

APARTMENT BLOCKS

Most people in the city of Rome were very poor. They lived in small, overcrowded flats in blocks up to six storeys tall. Many of these buildings were made with cheap materials and they often collapsed. Fires were common and people were trapped on the upper floors. There were no toilets except on the ground floor. Water had to be carried upstairs. There was no glass in the windows to keep the cold out.

Glass was very rare and expensive until glassblowing was invented in the 1st century BCE.

Glassblowing
The ingredients for glass were heated to very hot in wood-fired kilns (ovens) then blown into shape by experienced glassblowers. They made jugs, vases, goblets and other vessels for kitchens.

Pots were made on a wheel or in a mould and then fired in kilns.

"I've made 12 pots today!"

CRAFTS
Most of the craftspeople in ancient Rome were men. Many were highly skilled and they made sculptures, pots, plates, bowls, vases, paintings, mosaics, jewellery and more. They usually learned their skills in small family workshops.

Pottery
Roman potters made vessels for preparing, serving, storing and transporting food, oil and drink. They also made lamps and perfume containers.

Fresh honey cakes today!

BAKERY

POTS & VASES

"Fresh honey cakes!"

Cups

Bottles

Plates and bowls

Amphorae

Bakers
Bakers sold white sourdough bread which they baked in hot ashes or earthenware ovens. Pastry cooks made cakes and other desserts sweetened with honey or grape juice.

Sourdough bread was a mix of flour and water. The dough was left in the open air and wild, airborne yeasts made it rise.

Potters
Brown earthenware pottery was used for everything, from containers for storing, cooking and serving food to household lamps and perfume bottles. The shops that sold pottery usually made it in a workshop at the back of the shop.

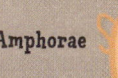

Amphorae were large jars used to carry and store liquid food items like olive oil, fish sauce and wine.

Storage jars

THE MERCHANT'S SON

During the Republic, the Romans exported goods and grew their food in the country around Rome. But by 100 CE, they were importing almost everything, from all over the empire and beyond. The city of Rome had no large industries or mass production, everything was made by hand. Its imports arrived at the port of Ostia, then came up the River Tiber.

SILVESTER

Hi! I'm Silvester. My father is a trader. He just came back from Africa with three lion cubs!

Traders made big money by importing wild animals like lions, tigers and elephants. They took part in the games at the Colosseum.

Luxury trade
There were only a few wealthy people in Roman times, but they were very rich indeed. They could afford silk from China and jewels from India, as well as perfumes, silver and fine glassware.

Lion cubs

What did they import?
By 100 CE Rome had more than one million inhabitants. To supply so many people all kinds of products had to be imported, from food and cloth to pots and pans.

Oil · Wine · Grain · Spices · Cloth · Gold, gemstones · Wood

Trade routes
The Romans traded mainly by sea. Transporting goods overland was too slow and expensive.

Banking
The first banks in Rome were located in temples. Merchants could borrow money to pay for cargo. Interest rates were very high but if the cargo was lost the bank had to pay.

Rich people and traders deposited their money in banks for safekeeping.

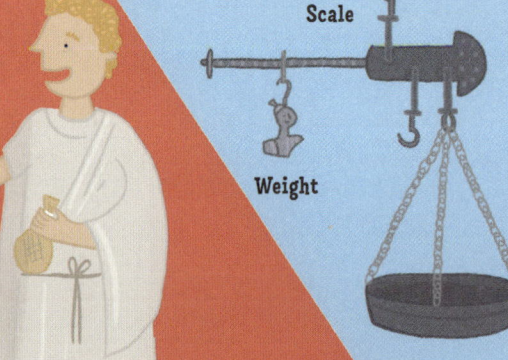

Scale · Weight

After a certain date Roman coins often showed a portrait of the emperor.

Weights and measures
Before the Romans began to use coins to pay for things, they used a system of bronze weights. This was quite impractical as everything had to be carefully weighed.

Money
The Romans first began using coins to pay for things in the 4th century BCE. Gradually they adopted a unified system that worked all over the empire, which greatly encouraged trade.

Roman coins

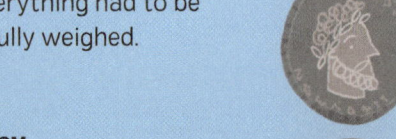

WHAT DID THEY TRADE?
Common trade items included grain from Egypt, Africa and the Crimea, metals and olive oil from Spain and Africa and silks and spices from India and the Far East.

The Chinese kept silk-making a secret for many years, until two monks smuggled silkworm eggs inside a bamboo pole to Constantinople.

The Romans met and clashed with the Celtic peoples in France and Britain for more than 500 years.

TRADING IDEAS TOO
The Romans traded far and wide, meeting and mixing with peoples at the edges of their ever-expanding empire, and beyond. The Romans were relatively open-minded in their dealings with other cultures. In many cases they listened and learned, and often adopted local gods and customs.

A Celtic warrior

Sea trade
Merchant ships varied greatly in size. They relied on square sails and oars, including steering oars. Merchants usually sailed their ships close to the coast and preferred to spend nights in port. Shipwrecks were common and pirates were also a menace.

Oh no! Look, Dad. Pirates!

Hello! I'm Sophia. I'm 17 and married to a rich merchant. This is our home.

SOPHIA

THE YOUNG WIFE

Family was very important to the Romans. Large, mixed family groups all lived together houses or flats. Wealthy families in Rome lived in large, comfortable villas like the one shown here. There was plenty of space for all the family, including grandparents, aunts, uncles and cousins.

Large cool gardens within the walls often had fountains.

Gardens

Fountain

Aristocratic and wealthy girls like Sophia married in their late teens.

It's bathtime. Into the tub you go!

Children
Sophia would be expected to have lots of children. If she didn't want to look after the children herself, she had maids, slaves and nannies to help.

Up until the age of seven, children were considered as infants and were cared for by women in the household.

Dining room

The dining room
The dining (or banqueting), room was an important space. Although the Romans had chair and stools to sit on, they preferred to lounge on couches at mealtimes, so they needed a lot of space.

The kitchen
Many smaller houses and flats did not have kitchens, but large homes like this one had a spacious area for cooking and preparing food. Rich Romans often gave banquets with many slaves, working under a head chef, preparing a huge feast.

Decoration
Rooms in wealthy homes were richly decorated with paintings, carvings and mosaics. Often, all the walls were covered with frescoes (paintings) of scenes or panels of colour. The floors were covered in mosaics (made by piecing together small cubes of coloured glass or stone). Mosaics were often designed in geometric black and white designs.

This mosaic tile from the ancient Roman town of Pompeii is inscribed Cave Canem which means "Beware of the Dog".

The Domus

A wealthy household with a large home (called a domus), usually included relatives and long-staying guests. These houses were run by the owner's wife. She gave the slaves or servants their daily orders, decided menus, and supervised the children and elderly members of the household, making sure that everything ran smoothly.

Bedrooms were usually small, and few members of the family had one of their own.

Bedrooms

A double-ended couch or bed like this one would have had a mattress, blankets and pillows to make it comfortable.

Couch

Footstool

Roofs were generally covered in terracotta tiles.

FURNITURE

Wealthy Romans owned elegant furniture, although to our eyes a Roman house would look underfurnished. Large pieces, like hefty wardrobes, were rare, as furniture needed to be light enough to move to summer houses in the country.

Shops

Our daughter-in-law Sophia takes good care of us.

Kitchen

The outer walls of the family home were often rented out to tradespeople who needed space for their shops and workshops.

Grandparents

Roman households were usually made up of several generations. Young wives like Sophia moved into their husband's family home where they were expected to help out with all the members of the family, including his elderly parents.

Older people were valued and respected in ancient Rome.

QUIZ TIME!

Have you read the whole book? How much can you remember? Answer these 20 questions to test your knowledge. Don't worry if you don't know all the answers. Skim through the pages again to find them. The answers are on page 44.

1. The Etruscan people lived in Italy before the Romans. They had an advanced society.

▲ TRUE
▽ FALSE

2. According to legend, Rome was founded by:

A. The Trojan hero Aeneas
B. Romulus and Remus
C. Etruscan kings
D. Leonardo da Vinci

3. During the Republic, Rome was ruled by kings.

▲ TRUE
▽ FALSE

4. The Romans fought the Punic Wars against:

A. The Greeks
B. The Etruscans
C. The Carthaginians
D. The British

5. Who was the first Roman Emperor?

A. Julius Caesar
B. Trajan
C. Augustus
D. Hadrian

6. Agriculture was the basis of wealth in the Roman world and most people worked as farmers.

▲ TRUE   ▽ FALSE

7. The Colosseum was built as a place to hold:

A. Religious ceremonies
B. Sporting events
C. Wedding ceremonies
D. Business meetings

8. The Pantheon is a large temple that still stands today in the city of Rome. It was built as a temple dedicated to all the gods and goddesses.

▲ TRUE   ▽ FALSE

9. Why was Hadrian's Wall built in the north of England?

A. To keep out fierce Celtic tribes from the north
B. As a tourist attraction
C. As a place for soldiers to meet up
D. To stop sheep from wandering north into Scotland

10. The Vestal Virgins were powerful priestesses in ancient Rome. Their main job was:

A. To hold parties and attend social gatherings
B. To keep the sacred flame of Rome alight
C. To hold sacrifices of sheep to honour the gods
D. To teach girls how to read

11. Saturnalia was the most important festival in the Roman calendar. During the celebration people greeted each other by saying "Io Saturnalia!" What did it mean?

A. Happy Holidays!
B. Let's have a party!
C. Saturn is a big planet
D. I'm going to a banquet

12. The Romans were very good at building:

A. Roads
B. Drains and sewers
C. Aqueducts
D. All of the above

13. Charioteers were often slaves or from poor families who became immensely rich by racing their chariots in front of huge crowds.

▲ TRUE
▽ FALSE

14. There were many slaves in ancient Rome. Usually they were people who had been taken prisoner during a war.

▲ TRUE   ▽ FALSE

15. Which sentence is true:

A. Rome was a small, quiet town with just a few inhabitants
B. Rome was a huge, noisy city packed with people

16. What language did the Romans speak?
A. Italian
B. Latin
C. French
D. Gaelic

17. Jupiter, Juno and Minerva were the three main gods and goddesses of ancient Rome.

▲ TRUE   ▽ FALSE

18. The Romans transported goods mainly by sea and pirates were a constant menace.

▲ TRUE   ▽ FALSE

19. Wealthy Roman women were expected to:

A. Have lots of children
B. Run large households
C. Take care of all family members
D. All of the above

20. All Romans lived in large luxurious villas.

▲ TRUE   ▽ FALSE

INDEX

A
Aemilia, Vestal, 18
Apulia 8
Augustus, Emperor 11, 14, 15

B
bakers 33
banking 34
Baths of Caracalla 26-27
butchers 32
Byzantine Empire 6, 15

C
Caligula, Emperor 14
Carthage 10
Celts 35
charioteers 24
Cicero 31
Circus Maximus 7, 25
clothing 28, 29
Coelia Concordia, Vestal, 18
Colosseum 7, 15
Commodus, Emperor 14
Constantinople 6

D
Diocletian, Emperor 6
Domitian, Emperor 14

E, F
Etruscans 8-9
feast days 20
food 13
founding of Rome 6, 9

G
Gaius Appuleius 25
gladiators 15, 32
glassblowers 33
Greeks 8, 22

H
Hadrian, Emperor 14, 15
Hadrian's Wall 16
hairstyles 28
Hannibal 10
Hypatia 31

J
jewellery 29
Julius Caesar 11
Juno, goddess, 21
Jupiter, god, 21

L
Latins 8
lawyers 30-31
Livy 31

M
Minerva, goddess, 21
money 34

Nero, Emperor 14

O
Odoacer 6
olive oil 12
Ostia 34

P
Pantheon 6, 7, 21
pirates 35
pottery 33
Punic Wars 10

R
Remus 6, 9
Rhea Silvia, Vestal, 18
roads 21
Romulus 6, 9

S, T
schools 30
slavery 28
Trajan, Emperor 14, 15, 16

U, V W
Umbri 8
Venice 8
Vesta, goddess, 18
Vestal virgins 18-19
Virgil 31
women's education 30

ANSWERS TO THE QUIZ
(on pages 42-43)

1	True	8	True	15	B
2	B	9	A	16	B
3	False	10	B	17	True
4	C	11	A	18	True
5	C	12	D	19	C
6	True	13	True	20	False
7	B	14	True		

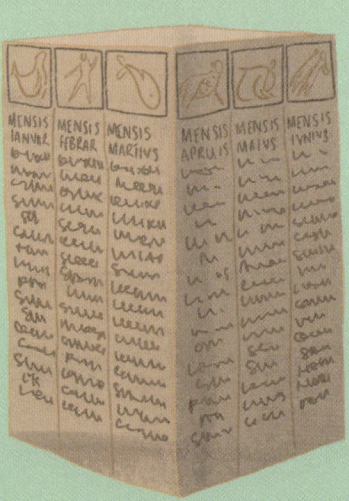

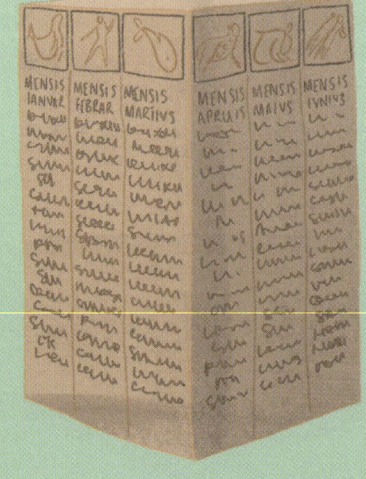